Once Upon an Elephant

by Linda Stanek

illustrated by Shennen Bersani

Once upon an elephant, the sun beat down on the hot, cracked earth. Rivers ran dry. The animals of the savannah risked dying from thirst.

But the elephants were there.

They dug in the riverbanks with their tusks. They cracked the hard soil, shoveled through mud, and reached water. And the animals gathered 'round and drank.

Once upon an elephant, the forest's trees grew thick and strong. Some trees sprouted in the grasslands and threatened to turn the area into a forest.

But the elephants were there.

They wrapped strong trunks around the
sprouts and saplings. They plucked them out
and ate them. So gazelles sprinted through
the open fields. Lions stalked in the tall grass.
And mongoose hunted and ate.

Once upon an elephant, animals needed
salt that was hidden in the ground.

But the elephants were there.

They sensed the salt and gouged away the dirt. They ate trunkfuls of the salty dirt to get the minerals. And antelope, zebra, and baboons licked the salt too, so they grew quick, healthy, and strong.

Once upon an elephant, the seeds dropped from the trees in pods so thick they could not sprout.

But the elephants were there.

They ate the seeds. When the seeds passed
through them, the pods thinned and then could
sprout. The elephant's dung gave the sprouts food,
and they grew into tall, wide trees. The forest trees
gave shade to the animals on the ground, and a
place for birds to nest.

Once upon an elephant, small animals far from the rivers were thirsty.

But the elephants were there.

Their deep footprints caught water when it rained,
forming tiny pools. And mice drank, frogs croaked,
and insects hummed and buzzed.

Once upon an elephant, lightning crackled through the sky, striking the dry savannah. With a snap and a sizzle, a lick of flame rose in the grass. The fire grew and raced through the grassland.

But the elephants were there.

Over the years, they had trekked through the brush, forming wide paths where few plants grew. The fire that reached those paths could slow or even stop if there wasn't enough wind to push the flames to the other side. So the zebras, foxes, and leopards that raced across the elephant paths had a chance to get away.

Once upon an elephant, people knew that someday soon all elephants might die. If that happened—if the elephants became extinct— people would have to say that elephants were only *once upon a time.*

But for now . . .

Once upon an elephant, the moon shone from the star-speckled sky. Mothers wrapped trunks around sleepy calves. And the big, dark world felt good and right as the elephants fell asleep.

For Creative Minds

Keystone Species

An ecosystem is made of all the living and non-living things in an area. A savanna is one type of ecosystem. Savannas are usually found between a desert and a forest. Savannas are made of grass with a few trees and bushes. They have a warm climate with a rainy season and a dry season. There are savannas all around the world. Many savannas are in Africa.

All the living things in an ecosystem are connected. Sometimes there is one species that plays an important role in the ecosystem. This is called a **keystone species**. A keystone species helps other living things meet their basic needs. If something happens to a keystone species, the whole ecosystem is hurt. In the African savanna, elephants are a keystone species.

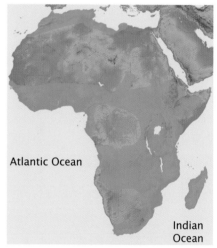

Savannas in Africa

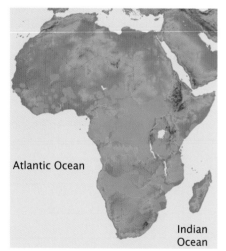

Elephant habitats in Africa

Elephants used to live across all of Africa south of the Sahara desert. Now the places where they can live (habitats) are shrinking. People build new cities and roads, use savannas for farmland, and cut down forests. There are fewer wild places for elephants to live. This is called habitat loss.

In many places, elephants are killed illegally for their ivory tusks. This is called poaching. Poachers kill elephants so they can cut off their tusks and sell them.

Elephants are a vulnerable species because of habitat loss and poaching. People need to help protect the elephants. Without our help, elephants could disappear forever (become extinct).

Rainy Season, Dry Season

In many tropical habitats, there are only two seasons: the rainy season and the dry season. Sort the following events based on whether they occur in the rainy season or the dry season.

A. Plants need water to grow. When rain falls on the seeds in elephants' dung, the seeds sprout.

B. Fire burns the dry grass. The fire spreads quickly until it is slowed by the elephant path.

C. Animals need water to live. Elephants dig into dry earth to find water underneath.

D. Rain gathers in the elephants' footprints. Animals drink out of the small puddles.

Rainy season: A and D. Dry season: B and C.

All About Elephants

Female: cow
Male: bull
Baby: calf
Group name: herd

Elephants are the largest land animal on earth.

Cows usually live in family groups. The oldest or highest-ranking female leads the herd.

Elephants eat only plants (herbivores). They spend 16 hours a day eating or looking for food.

Bulls leave the herd when they are young. They live alone or with other bulls.

Elephants usually live into their early forties. Some elephants can live for 50 years or longer.

Wild elephants weigh up to 14,000 lbs (6,350 kg). That is as heavy as a school bus!

To Mom and Dad with love. Special thanks to Harry Peachey for inspiring this book and for guidance and support along the way.—LS

While doing research for my illustrations, I visited Alice, Ginny, and Kate—the amazing African elephants at the Roger Williams Park Zoo in Providence, RI. Then I trekked back to Boston to visit the Franklin Park Zoo's lion.   Both zoos bring a piece of Africa home to New Englanders by showcasing large numbers of African wildlife. My heartfelt thanks to Lou Marcoccio for joining me on these "safari" adventures, and Cynthia Germain for her inspirational African jewelry. And, as always, thanks to my loving family for supporting my safari. In memory of my friend and fellow author, Michael Palmer, MD.—SB

Thanks to the International Elephant Foundation for reviewing the accuracy of the information in this book.

Library of Congress Cataloging-in-Publication Data

Names: Stanek, Linda, author. | Bersani, Shennen, illustrator.
Title: Once upon an elephant / by Linda Stanek ; illustrated by Shennen
    Bersani.
Description: Mount Pleasant, SC : Arbordale Publishing, [2016] | Audience:
    Ages 4-8. | Includes bibliographical references. | Description based on
    print version record and CIP data provided by publisher; resource not
    viewed.
Identifiers: LCCN 2015038095 (print) | LCCN 2015037682 (ebook) | ISBN
    9781628557527 (English Download) | ISBN 9781628557664 (Eng. Interactive) |
    ISBN 9781628557596 (Spanish Download) | ISBN 9781628557732 (Span.
    Interactive) | ISBN 9781628557312 (english hardcover) | ISBN 9781628557381
    (english pbk.) | ISBN 9781628557527 (english downloadable ebook) | ISBN
    9781628557664 (english interactive dual-language ebook) | ISBN
    9781628557459 (spanish pbk.) | ISBN 9781628557596 (spanish downloadable
    ebook) | ISBN 9781628557732 (spanish interactive dual-language ebook)
Subjects: LCSH: Elephants--Juvenile literature. |
    Elephants--Ecology--Juvenile literature. | Animal ecology--Juvenile
    literature. | Keystone species--Juvenile literature. | Savanna
    ecology--Juvenile literature.
Classification: LCC QL737.P98 (print) | LCC QL737.P98 S725 2016 (ebook) | DDC
    599.67--dc23
LC record available at http://lccn.loc.gov/2015038095

Translated into Spanish by Rosalyna Toth: *Erase un elefante*
Lexile® Level: AD 730
keywords: Africa, elephant, grassland/savanna, habitat/animal interaction, keystone species

Bibliography:

African Elephant Conservation Act. Summary Report 1998-2000. Washington DC: U.S. Department of the Interior, 2001. Print.
Elephants. San Francisco: Fog City Press, 2010. Print.
Felts, Adam, Head keeper of elephants at the Columbus Zoo and Aquarium. (2009, November 9). Personal interview.
Kalman, Bobbie. Endangered Elephants: Earth's Endangered Animal Series. New York: Crabtree Publishing Company, 2005. Print.
"Keystone Species," http://www.nature.com/scitable/knowledge/library/keystone- species-15786127. National Geographic Education,
    2013. Web. December 12, 2013.
"Mammals: Elephant." http://animals.sandiegozoo.org/animals/elephant. San Diego Zoo Animals, 2013. Web. December 2, 2013.
Morgan, Jody. Elephant Rescue: Changing the Face of Endangered Wildlife. Firefly Animal Rescue Series. Richmond Hill, Ontario: Firefly
    Books, 2004.
Munscher, Eric. "Understanding the Role of Keystone Species in Their Ecosystems." http://www.swca.com/index.php/media/newsdetail/
    understanding-the-role-of-keystone-species-in-their-ecosystems/SWCA Environmental Consultants, 2013. Web. December 6, 2013.
Peachey, Harry, Curator of Columbus Zoo and Aquarium and Board Member of the International Elephant Foundation. (2013, December
    16). Personal Interview.
Wagner, Stephen C. "Keystone Species." http://www.nature.com/scitable/knowledge/library/keystone-species-15786127. Nature
    Education, 2012. Web. November 12, 2013.

Manufactured in China, June 2017
This product conforms to CPSIA 2008
Second Printing

Arbordale Publishing
Mt. Pleasant, SC 29464
www.ArbordalePublishing.com